PUBLISHED IN 2020 BY
FIREWORK PUBLISHING

COPYRIGHT 'ILLUSTRATIONS' 2020 FIREWORK PUBLISHING
ALL RIGHT RESERVED.'NO PART OF THIS PUBLICATION MAY BE REPRODUCED OR TRANSMITTED IN ANY
FORM OR BY ANY MEANS, ELECTRONIC OR MECHANICAL, INCLUDING PHOTOCOPY RECORDING OR ANY
INFORMATION STORAGE SYSTEM AND RETRIEVAL SYSTEM WITHOUT PERMISSION IN WRITING
BY FIREWORK PUBLISHING

PRINTED IN THE UNITED STATE OF AMERICA

This book belongs to
_____

www.ingramcontent.com/pod-product-compliance
Lightning Source LLC
LaVergne TN
LVHW062332220225
804339LV00026B/693